This book belongs to:

_____

C153704314

A catalogue record for this book is available from the British Library

Published by Ladybird Books Ltd
80 Strand London WC2R ORL
A Penguin Company

2 4 6 8 10 9 7 5 3 1
© LADYBIRD BOOKS LTD MMVIII
LADYBIRD and the device of a Ladybird are trademarks of Ladybird Books Ltd

ISBN: 978-1-84646-936-7

Printed in China

My best book about....

Wild Animals

Written by Mandy Ross
Illustrated by Kate and Liz Pope

Look at all these wild animals!
Which ones are big and heavy?
Which ones are small?

Some wild animals run fast.

Some get around in other ways.
Can you jump like a kangaroo?

Some animals live where it's hot.
How many monkeys can you spot?

These animals live where it's cold.

Which ones have fur to keep them warm?

At the river, lots of animals come for a splash or a cool drink.

Can you snap your hands like
a crocodile's mouth?

We're off on a trip to spot wild animals. Can you show the jeep which way to go to find the elephants?

What do these animals eat?
Would you like to eat this kind
of food?

Some animals have sharp teeth
and claws... or tusks, or beaks.
How many teeth have you got?

A tail is a useful thing.

So is a trunk! What are these elephants using their trunks for?

Some animals have patterns to help them hide – or for showing off!

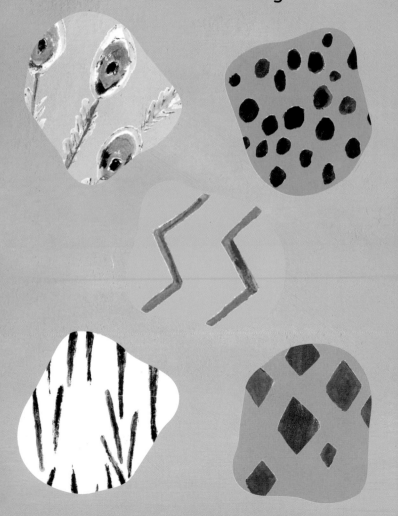

Can you match the animals to their patterns?

Wild animals need a comfortable, safe place to sleep.
Would you like to sleep like this?

Can you make these animal noises?

Trumpety-trump!

Roar!

Which wild animals do you like best?

Hoo-hoo-hoo!

Snap, snap!

Sssss!

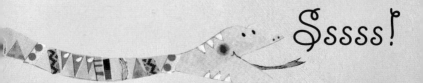

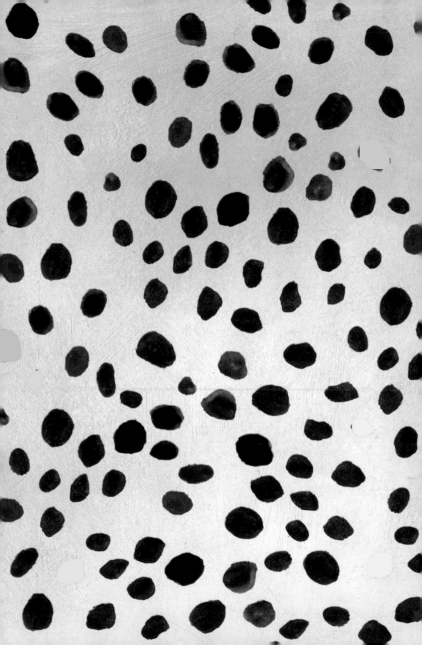